J. S. (John Saul) Howson

Sacramental Confession

J. S. (John Saul) Howson

Sacramental Confession

ISBN/EAN: 9783742857057

Manufactured in Europe, USA, Canada, Australia, Japa

Cover: Foto ©ninafisch / pixelio.de

Manufactured and distributed by brebook publishing software (www.brebook.com)

J. S. (John Saul) Howson

Sacramental Confession

CONTENTS.

CHAP.	PAGE
I. INTRODUCTORY	1
II. DEFINITION	15
III. MORTAL AND VENIAL SIN	29
IV. THE BIBLE: CONFESSION TO MAN	42
V. THE BIBLE: CONFESSION TO GOD	53
VI. CHURCH HISTORY	68
VII. THE CHURCH OF ENGLAND	81
VIII. ORDINATION AND ABSOLUTION	96
IX. PRACTICAL RESULTS	113

CHAPTER I.

INTRODUCTORY.

A SLIGHT glance at the chapters which compose this book will show that it is intended merely for popular use. Elaborate arguments on the subject to which they relate I leave to those who have more leisure: exhaustive historical treatment of the subject to those who have larger learning. This is a question which can be dealt with very usefully without the possession of the two great advantages of leisure and learning. The Confessional Controversy is not like the Eucharistic Controversy, for instance, which can hardly be treated adequately without touching on metaphysical subtleties, or without some considerable research. The doctrine and practice of Sacramental Confession are in immediate and well-understood contact with our social and domestic life: they have certain broad general features, easily elucidated from Holy Scripture and from History; and practical issues are raised by them, which can be stated very clearly, and can be readily apprehended by any person of ordinary intelligence.

That the question before us has deeply moved the public mind in England is quite evident; nor is it at all likely that general interest in the subject will speedily decay. Those who desire to re-introduce into the Church of England the theory and habit of Sacramental Confession are conspicuously in earnest; and, meanwhile, the meetings held in reference to this matter in various parts of the country, whatever be the value of the utterances made on such occasions, have shown very clearly that the utmost repugnance is widely felt to the efforts which are diligently made by some of our Clergy, with the acquiescence of some of our Laity, to bring back amongst us a discarded system.

When any religious topic thus largely pervades the general mind, and is productive everywhere of uneasy thoughts, if Clergymen who hold positions of special responsibility are silent regarding it, they create the impression that they are glad to evade that which is the main point for the moment, and that they are wanting in proper courage. At such a time the people at large look to the Clergy, if not for guidance, at least for information. Our chief guidance indeed must come, of course, from the Bishops; and we have reason to express gratitude for several Episcopal statements on the subject, which are prudent and moderate on the one hand, and explicit and reassuring on the other. But all who are in the ministerial office have their duty too in reference to these matters; and especially they are bound to call to mind that ordination-vow which pledges them to use their best endeavours to "drive away" doctrines alien to the religious system which "this Church and Realm hath received."[*] Under these circumstances I have felt it to be right to preach on this subject in Chester Cathedral, and now to publish the substance of my sermons, with additions and improvements, after well weighing what has appeared in the local press on the other side, and indeed on many sides, of the subject.[†]

This being an introductory chapter, it is convenient that I should state in it more fully, once for all, my reasons and excuses for such preaching and such publishing.

I regard these diligent efforts for the re-introduction of the Confessional System amongst us as one of the most serious parts of that great aggressive movement, which one of our Bishops has justly called a "counter-reformation." This movement, at the point which it has now reached, no longer derives its strength from its earlier principle

---

[*] "The Form and Manner of ordering Priests."

[†] A similar reference might with equal justice have been made to the local newspapers of any neighbourhood in the country; and no stronger proof could be given of the prevailing uneasiness to which the subject has given rise.

—that the Primitive Church ought to be kept before us as our model. Many of our Clergy have now palpably placed themselves under the teaching of the Modern Church of Rome. The manuals of that Church are largely used in private, to supply materials for the public instruction of the people. New habits of thought are, by such methods, gradually made familiar. New phraseology from this source is successfully infiltrated into our current divinity. This is peculiarly the case in respect of the subject before us. The very use of the phrase, "Sacramental Confession,"* will be seen, by any one who really understands the meaning of the phrase, to be an indication of the grave change that is coming over us.

I know it will be said that there is injustice in this way of stating the question—that there is a Roman and an Anglican view of the

* In illustration of the bold use of this term by those who have signed our twenty-fifth article, it is enough to refer to the notorious petition of the 483, and to an article which appeared in the " Contemporary Review " for November, 1873.

Confessional, and that it is not fair to confuse the two together as though they were identical; and many of those who use this language are perfectly sincere. But I am old enough to recollect very similar expostulations, which it was necessary afterwards to withdraw. Not very many years ago the teaching of the Earlier Church was presented to us as that under the shadow of which alone we could understand the New Testament; and arguments to this effect were used in combination with vehement protestations against Romanism: but in due time, under such influences and after such protestations, we lost, and Rome gained, a considerable part of the flower of our Clergy. How well I remember meeting Frederick Faber one day in the streets of Edinburgh, about the time when the ninetieth of the "Tracts for the Times" was published, and asking him whether he did not think that Romanism was the inevitable issue of the progress which had then been made; to which his reply was to this effect, that joining the Church of Rome was the one thing most impossible. I am quite sure that he was sincere; but we all know the later history of that attractive, but most admonitory life. And as with him, so with many others of both sexes. Those who have learnt to listen for the teaching of "the Church," as the one voice which is to guide them, will be very apt to grow dissatisfied with indistinct echoes coming to them confusedly from remote early times, and to crave for an ever-present Church which gives immediate directions for the wants of the moment. Men and women, whose minds have been attuned to Roman teaching, are likely to become impatient of many things within our own Church which must jar upon their feelings like discord. What has happened before may happen again; and especially is this probability great in connection with such practical matters as Confession and Absolution. When these risks are very present to the mind, it is hardly possible to be silent.

Here a remark must be permitted, which I am anxious so to express as to give no unnecessary pain and offence. Our danger is much increased by the influence of party-spirit. Reference has been made above to some (probably not a very large number) who see clearly the end towards which they are moving, and who, in pursuing this end, display the utmost vigilance, tact, and perseverance.* Others (I hope they are still fewer) are not very scrupulous in their methods of promoting what they desire.† But with

---

* In a volume of "The Evangelist Library," edited by the Mission Priests of St. John the Evangelist, I find such phrases as the following:—" The majority of our people have a great dislike to *Sacramental Confession*. . . . . . The Mission priest should be careful to explain that, when he invites persons to come and see him on spiritual matters, it is not simply for confession, but to assist those who do not wish to confess. . . . When he finds the Mission ripe for it, he will give notice that he will begin to hear confessions. . . . . . The priest, having gained as good a knowledge as he can of the spiritual condition of his visitor, will, in most cases, have to recommend confession as desirable, if not necessary, for him."—*Parochial Missions*, ch. v.

† Several copies have reached me, by post, of a paper entitled "Information on Confession," and professing to give a *catena* of Church of England authorities for the practice. Among these authorities is the Church Catechism. When St. Paul wrote, "Let a man *examine himself*, and so let him eat of that bread and drink of that cup," what would he have thought of

such persons others, who differ from them extremely, are associated by party ties, which they have not the courage to break. A small body of extreme men can be made very strong and very dangerous by the apparent union along with them, under some common designation, of large numbers, who are really not at one with them at heart. We sometimes see this fact made very evident in political combinations; and what is true in the world of politics, is equally true in the ecclesiastical world. I will venture to express my meaning by asking a very pointed question: Is it right for "moderate High Churchmen" to keep aloof from "Evangelicals," whom they are tempted to dislike, but of whom they probably know very little, and to connect themselves, in all that attracts the public eye, with those from whom they really differ far more seriously? And is it not reasonable to hope that this question of

any one who should have interpreted the sentence to mean, "Let a man *confess to a priest*, and so let him eat of that bread and drink of that cup?"

"Sacramental Confession," at the height which it has now attained, may become the occasion for a braver and more consistent attitude, and for some plain speaking on behalf of the true interests of the Church of England?

Another argument, however, will be used, and quite sincerely, to deprecate the writing of a controversial book of this kind. It will be said that among those who are the most extreme in their view of the value of customary private Confession, and customary private Absolution, there is a vast amount of admirable work among the poor, and of high religious devotion. This fact is not at all denied: it is most thankfully acknowledged; but it does not in the least degree alter the duty of speaking and writing strongly against that which is felt to be erroneous and perilous. On the contrary, it makes this duty all the more imperative. In the course of the history of the Church, some of the most serious deviations from right doctrine and sound practice have been helped forward by their association with men of high and devoted character. Will any one question the earnest missionary exertion, the patient pastoral care, which are found within the Church of Rome itself? But does it follow that the decrees of the Council of Trent are in harmony with Holy Scripture? Will any one question the wide benevolence and generous giving of many Unitarians? But does it follow that our Blessed Redeemer is not Divine? Perhaps when the present period in the annals of the Church of England is read hereafter, it will be seen that some of our most pressing dangers had been closely connected with names worthy of the utmost honour.

For the reasons thus briefly stated, this volume takes the form of protest and controversy against the position of the Church of Rome. *There* is the shore towards which this current of English feeling is really moving: *there* "Sacramental Confession" is found in its mature form and consolidated strength; and *thence* even now the chief instruction on the subject among ourselves within the Church of England is fetched. It is indeed quite possible that absolute defections from our own fold to the Roman are not to be apprehended so much as heretofore. The decree of Papal Infallibility, combined with the Syllabus, may possibly have made a gulf where formerly stood a bridge. But if we place ourselves under the teaching of the Modern Church of Rome, almost as much harm may be done as though large numbers of our people were to join that communion. Perhaps one of the evils, which we have most reason to dread within our own communion, is "Popery without the Pope."

At all events, there is a state of thought and feeling among ourselves at this time, in reference to the Confessional, very similar to that state of thought and feeling, in the earlier Christian ages, which gradually led to the system of Compulsory Auricular Confession. Of that system it was said by Bishop Blomfield, in his celebrated Charge of 1842, that it is a practice "utterly unknown to the Primitive Church, one of the most fearful abuses of that of Rome, and the source of unspeakable abominations."* I propose to take these words of a distinguished and most sagacious prelate as a kind of text to be commented on in the following pages. If the sentence is even approximately true, it becomes us to weigh most seriously our existing attitude in regard to this question.

As to the present position of the Anglican Church in reference to this subject, we are now in what may be called the Romance of the Confessional; and it cannot be out of place to invite attention to its sober and sad realities. The whole matter, with us, at present, is incipient; and it is well to show what "Sacramental Confession" really is in its maturity. I can quite understand the attractiveness of the flowers in early spring; but of far greater importance is the ripe fruit in the late autumn. My conviction is that, in the present case, the fruit on the whole is unwholesome and bad. In expressing

* "Charge to the Clergy of the Diocese of London." October 1842, p. 57.

this strongly, and endeavouring to prove it, I hope I shall write without giving needless pain, without deviating from candour and courtesy, and without forgetting that the promoters of a mischievous system may themselves be honourable and earnest men.

CHAPTER II.

DEFINITION.

THE subject of this book is "Auricular Confession," or "Sacramental Confession;" and I am desirous not to be drawn aside from this main subject into any collateral topic. Moreover, popular misapprehensions are widely prevalent regarding the exact meaning of at least the second of these phrases. I will therefore employ the pages of this chapter chiefly for the purposes of definition.

As to the former phrase, used by Bishop Blomfield in the sentence quoted near the end of the preceding chapter, only a very slight explanation can be needed. The word "auricular" is a Latin word, though it belongs rather to ecclesiastical, than to classical Latin. It denotes that which has strictly and exclusively to do with the ear. That part of medical science, which is limited to this organ, would properly be called auricular. That confession of sin, which is told privately into the ear of the priest, and to no one else, is auricular. The great feature of this kind of confession is that it is strictly *confidential*. Where this system is the Church's rule, so as to pervade the community, the Priest knows what the wife does not tell to her husband, what the daughter does not tell to her mother. He knows more concerning crime than can be known to the magistrate. In the high places of the world he is in possession of State secrets. He is acquainted likewise with thoughts and desires, which have never found utterance, except in such confession. This minute acknowledgment, too, of sin in thought, word, and deed, is made in the conviction that the priest has the power of dealing with it *judicially*. Hence his dominion over the conscience, his opportunities of directing and controlling, are enormous, and yet absolutely secret.

I am not at this moment saying how far this system is desirable, or the contrary: certainly not doubting that there must be, and ought to be, confidential communication between Pastor and People. One of our own canons enjoins that "if any man confess his secret and hidden sins to the Minister, for the unburdening of his conscience, and to receive spiritual consolation and ease of mind from him," secrecy is to be observed by that Minister.[*] I am only illustrating the force of the word "auricular," and pointing out the tremendous importance of the subject as shown by the mere use of this word. Through the ear every priest may become a king.

And before we quit this topic, let another most serious aspect of it be remembered in passing. Such secrets are not secrets for ever. When He comes again, who is King over all, then, whatever confessions have been made

[*] Can. 113.

at any time—confessions of old men, of young women, of saints, of sinners—all will become publicly known. "For there is nothing covered that shall not be revealed; neither hid, that shall not be known. Whatsoever ye have spoken *in darkness* shall be heard in the light; and that which ye have spoken *in the ear* shall be proclaimed upon the housetops." *

But now we must turn to that other phrase, which is more to our present purpose, which is still more technical, and which, while the former phrase is clear enough, is itself, I imagine, often misunderstood. Many persons in England probably suppose that "Sacramental Confession" merely means the act or the habit of confessing before taking part in the *Sacrament* of the Lord's Supper. I dare say that some who will read these pages believe that nothing more is denoted by the term than an extension of what we find in one of the exhortations in the Prayer-Book. There it is said that, inasmuch as it is requisite that no one should come to the

* Luke xii. 2, 3.

Lord's Table but "with a full trust in God's mercy, and with a quiet conscience," if by private self-examination this state of mind cannot be attained, and "further comfort and counsel is required," then let such a person "come to some discreet and learned Minister of God's Word, and open his grief, that by the Ministry of God's Holy Word he may receive the benefit of absolution, together with ghostly counsel or advice, to the quieting of his conscience." * It is supposed by many, I say, that if that which is here set forth as exceptional, were to become the rule, then we should have "Sacramental Confession" in the Church of England.

Even this would be a very serious change. Hardly any change can be more serious, in matters of religion, than to turn an exception into a rule.† When a bottle is distinctly

---

* First Exhortation in the "Order of the Administration of the Lord's Supper."

† The exceptional nature of such communications between the penitent and the priest is made unequivocally manifest in the "Service for the Visitation of the Sick," by the phrases "if he

labelled "medicine," and when you remove the label, and persuade people that the contents of the bottle are wholesome and nutritious food, useful for all persons under all circumstances, you have at least assumed a very grave responsibility. But this is not what is meant by "Sacramental Confession." The phrase denotes something totally different. Those who wish to re-introduce the thing amongst us know full well what is meant by the term; and it is right that the English people should know it too.

What then is Sacramental Confession?

Conspicuous among the seven sacraments, in the doctrinal and practical system of the Church of Rome, is *the Sacrament of Penance* ; and of this Sacrament "Confession" is an essential part. The Sacrament of Penance consists of three parts—first, contrition of heart;[*] secondly, confession to a priest;

---

feel his conscience troubled with any weighty matter," and "if he humbly and heartily desire it."

[*] The alternative of *attrition*, which seems to me a parody of repentance, must not be altogether passed by. According to the theory which is expressed by this word, a priest's absolution

thirdly, absolution by a priest. The view which is inculcated and acted upon is this, that for sin after Baptism the Sacrament of Penance is the appointed remedy, and that of this sacrament private confession to a priest, with the view of obtaining his private absolution, is an essential part.

This, then, is the "Sacramental Confession" with which we have to deal; and in dealing with it all exaggeration must be avoided. Want of candour and want of care are sure, in the end, to weaken a controversial position. I will limit myself entirely to three sentences which are found in the Canons of the Council of Trent. That is an authority which cannot be gainsayed. For if it were alleged—which, considering the historical circumstances of the case, is hardly likely—that these Canons rest rather on the voice of a pope than that of the Church, yet now it has been ruled that the pope, speaking

may convey forgiveness, when sorrow for sin is merely a sense of its consequences, without any resolution to sin no more. See Dean Hook's "Church Dictionary."

officially on a question of faith or morals, is infallible; and if one pope is infallible, all popes in past time have been infallible; and if ever a pope spoke officially, it must have been in adopting the results of that great Council of Trent, which in fact, up to 1870, defined the position of the Modern Church of Rome.

The first of these sentences is as follows: "If any one shall deny that Sacramental Confession was instituted by Divine right, or that by Divine right it is necessary to salvation, or shall say that the manner of secretly confessing to a priest alone, which the Church Catholic hath always observed from the beginning, and doth observe, is alien from the institution and command of Christ, and is invented by man, let him be accursed."* Now let this sentence be looked at very carefully, and each word of it well weighed, that the amount of truth or error which it contains may be accurately measured. I appeal to any candid member of the Church of Eng-

* Sess. xiv. De Pœn. Can. 6.

land, well acquainted with his Bible and moderately well acquainted with Church History, to say whether this sentence does not contain five distinct deviations from truth.

First, Sacramental Confession was not instituted by Divine right. You cannot point to any command given by Christ to this effect. He did appoint Baptism and the Lord's Supper; and we see how the commands were understood by the fact that they were observed. But He did not appoint this at all; and nothing of this kind was observed. If you say that, when He gave to Peter the keys of the kingdom of heaven,*—or when He extended a commission of the same kind to all the Apostles,†—or when He breathed on the general body of the disciples, with those solemn words concerning the Holy Ghost and the retaining and remitting of sins,‡— He then instituted *secret compulsory auricular confession*, you assume the very point which requires to be proved. There is not the slightest evidence that the Apostles under-

* Matt. xvi. 19.   † Matt. xviii. 18.   ‡ John xx. 22, 23.

stood Him to mean this, but very strong evidence to the contrary.

Secondly, as to the assertion that the observance of this kind of confession is necessary to salvation—how do you account for the absolute silence of St. Paul on this subject, both in what he says and writes to Christians in general, and when he addresses those who are in the clerical office?

Thirdly, as to the assertion that what is observed by the Roman Catholic Church now was observed by the Catholic Church from the beginning, this is obviously incorrect. The characteristic of the system of the Modern Church of Rome is that Sacramental Confession is *imperative;* but we can give the very date of the edict which made it imperative. Let me now simply add, in regard to the sentence just quoted from the Canons of the Council of Trent, that, from what has been already said, it follows, fourthly, that Sacramental Confession is alien from the institution and command of Christ; and, fifthly, that it has been invented by man.

The second of the two sentences to be adduced from the Canons of the Council of Trent is this:—"If any one shall say that in the Sacrament of Penance for the remission of sins, it is not by Divine right necessary to confess all and singular mortal sins, which can be recalled by a careful exercise of memory, even if they be secret sins—and moreover, the circumstances which modify the character of sin—let him be accursed."* To the distinction between mortal and venial sins I shall recur in the next chapter. But we see immediately the power which this distinction gives to the priest; and this prepares us for the third quotation from these same Canons:—"If any one shall say that the sacramental absolution of a priest is not a judicial act, but merely the ministerial act of pronouncing and declaring the remission of his sins to the person confessing, if only he believes that he is absolved, let him be accursed."† Not a ministerial, but a judicial act! Let the reader weigh well this distinc-

* Sess. xiv. De Pœn. Can. 7.   † Ib., Can. 9.

tion with himself. Combined with what has been brought forward above concerning the necessity of Confession, it presents to us a power far more colossal and crushing than any other that can be named. We are accustomed to consider the Apostles as placed at the highest point of the Christian Ministry: but contrast such language with that used concerning himself by St. Paul, who tells those to whom he writes, concerning a case of public church-discipline and public church-censure, that he has not "dominion over their faith," but is "the helper of their joy"!*

And here, as regards this judicial position claimed by the Roman Catholic Clergy, let me ask that the matter may be viewed thus. When we read in the Scripture those many passages concerning the pardon of the penitent and believing sinner, can we doubt that he is immediately forgiven, when repentance is sincere and faith is truly exercised? Does any man who believes the Bible doubt this? If then the Judge of all men has forgiven,

* 2 Cor. i. 24.

where is the judicial function of the minister? Who would take an offender before the lower court, when he has already been acquitted in the higher?

These remarks may suffice for the purposes of definition, and for removing misconceptions. A desire has been strongly expressed that the system of Sacramental Confession should be re-introduced into the Church of England; and yet many members of that Church are not at all aware of what is meant by the term. We find both the phrase in its exact meaning, and the thing in its mature form, in the theology and the working of the Modern Church of Rome. I have referred, therefore, to the Canons of the Council of Trent. Of what has just been adduced from certain of those Canons, the following recapitulation may be useful. In these authoritative documents it is asserted or implied that man can distinguish between mortal and venial sin, the former being the sin which separates the soul eternally from God, the latter involving merely the pains of Purgatory; that all mortal sin which can be recalled in the memory must, with its attendant circumstances, in order to be forgiven, be privately confessed to a priest; that the priest's action in this matter is not ministerial, but judicial; that this system was divinely instituted at the beginning of our Holy Religion; that it has been continuously maintained and always put in practice by the Church ever since that time. Believing each one of these propositions to be untrue, I cannot but earnestly join the general protest against the restoration of a system resting on such a basis.

CHAPTER III.

MORTAL AND VENIAL SIN.

THE quotations given in the preceding chapter, from the Canons of the Council of Trent, show that the distinction between mortal and venial sins is closely and essentially connected with the question under discussion. Here we come across that which appears to me one of the most serious parts of the sacramental penitentiary system. To this distinction in its reference to this system I invite the most careful attention. It is really a vital point in the whole controversy. I will, therefore, limit the present chapter entirely to this subject.

The theoretical difference is very clearly

laid down in Roman Catholic Theology. Mortal Sin separates from the favour of God. Venial Sin does not. For Mortal Sin the penalty is Hell. For Venial Sin the penalty is Purgatory. Mortal Sin can only be forgiven through confession to a priest, and through receiving his absolution. Venial Sin it is not essential to confess, though for the soul's health it may be very desirable to do so. But how to distinguish between mortal and venial sin? A sin, which is venial under some circumstances, may become mortal under other circumstances. This momentous question can be decided only by a Priest who has been trained in Casuistical Divinity. The reader perceives at once the point to which all this leads up.

Let us first, however, look at this distinction in reference to its probable tendency to raise or to lower the standard of Christian moral feeling.

That all sins are equal in enormity, no one asserts. That there is the gravest difference between sins committed habitually, deliberately, and knowingly on the one hand, and sins committed through want of knowledge and through infirmity on the other, no one disputes. But the true seat of sin is in the heart. If the rules set before a sinner are tabulated human definitions—which, even if they were theoretically exact, must, in their application to any particular case, be liable to uncertainty, through human ignorance—will not the result be the creation of an artificial morality, extremely different in its method from what we find in the New Testament, and therefore unfavourable to the formation of Christian character? How can such a system be otherwise than unsound and dangerous? All sin is so dreadful in itself, so abhorrent to God, that it must be harmful to draw distinctions of this kind, especially if they run into minute detail. What we want is an instinctive, God-like abhorrence of all sin: and to divide sins theoretically into venial and mortal, curiously to study the fine and subtle lines by which the two classes can be discriminated, and practically to lead men to connect their hopes and fears with these distinctions, cannot be conducive to this holy God-like instinct.

But when this distinction of mortal sins from venial is used by a priesthood, whose office it is to decide for a sinner between temporary suffering and eternal separation from God, then a new element of the most terrible kind is introduced into the question. A system of confession and absolution, regulated according to such precarious lines of demarcation, and involving such dread alternatives, I cannot but regard as both cruel and deceiving; and with all my heart I must deprecate its re-introduction amongst us.

Anecdotes, which would be quite out of place in a sermon, are allowable here, especially as these pages, which are an amplification and re-arrangement of what was preached in Chester Cathedral, make no pretence to elaborate or learned treatment of the subject in hand. Anecdotes, too, are often very useful illustrations of a practical question of this kind. Nor need I make any apology for following the train of thought suggested, during a recent visit to the Continent, by intercourse with the "Old Catholics" of Germany and Switzerland. Moreover, uneasiness caused by this subject of Sacramental Confession is by no means limited to England. It is one of the causes of this very "Old Catholic" movement; and we shall probably hear of some serious discussions concerning it at the Synod to be held in Germany at Whitsuntide.

The recent Congress at Constance was held in the very room where John Huss was condemned to death; and the recollection of that great crime came up very freshly in the addresses of several of the speakers. It is said of John Huss, when on his way to be burnt, that he expressed a wish to confess to a priest. This was denied to him, except on the condition that he would first recant, or, in other words, would first give the lie to his honest convictions; on which he replied, "I am not guilty of mortal sin, and therefore confession is not essential."* This seems to me to illustrate forcibly, not only that distinguishing between mortal and venial sin, to which dogmatic authority was given at Trent, but also what I have called cruelty and deception in the Roman system of religion, and the terrible coherence with which its various parts hang together. Huss might have been in mortal sin; but he could not be delivered from Hell, except on condition of saying what was false. If at the last moment he had become a hypocrite, the gates of Heaven would have been thrown wide open to him.

I am reminded here of what a distinguished man said to me, a few months ago, of the putting of mere submission in the place of faith. His Bishop was one of those German Prelates who, before the Vatican Council, pronounced the Infallibility of the Pope to be untrue. On his return from the Council, he at first desired to resign his bishopric; but

* This story is given in Canon Robertson's "History of the Christian Church," vol. iv. p. 281.

the influence of the Jesuits was successfully exerted upon him; and then he required my informant, who himself held the same view, to give in his submission, on which this reply was given to the Bishop: "I read in the Bible, not of *submission*, but of *faith*: convince me that what you said was false last year is true this year, and I will thankfully yield."

During the same journey, I was once walking in Switzerland from one village to another with a priest, when our conversation fell upon the Confessional. I said to him, that I thought this system, based as it is upon the distinction between mortal and venial sin, is both cruel and deceiving. "Yes," he said, with a shrug of the shoulders; "and no one can draw the line between mortal and venial sin." Then he added, with another shrug, "*The Casuists can.*" On this I asked him what real effect resulted from the training of the Clergy on the casuistical method of Moral Theology. He answered, "It is the destruction of all religion." I ought to add that this man was at that time surrounded by the respect of his parishioners, and that he himself had been a professor in an Ecclesiastical Seminary.

For the sake of elucidating, to those who have not studied this subject, some characteristics of this system, I will state a case which by others will be recognised as familiar. Here is half-a-crown on a table. I desire to possess it, though it is not mine; and, no one seeing me, I appropriate it, or, in the plain honest language of the English people, I steal it. Now is this a mortal or a venial sin? "Here," say the Casuists, "*we must distinguish;* we must take into account to whom the half-crown belonged." So far as I can make out from Liguori,[*] whose moral theology is at present in very high honour and officially approved, the sin in his view would

---

[*] Prebendary Meyrick's "Moral and Devotional Theology of the Church of Rome, according to the Authoritative Teaching of S. Alfonso de' Liguori," published in 1857, ought to be well known and carefully studied. In one Diocese at least of our Sister Church in America, I observe that it is made a text-book for Theological Students.

be mortal if the coin were stolen from a beggar, but venial if it were stolen from a rich nobleman. Various opinions, however, on such a subject would be considered *probable*;* and yet we are concerned here with the tremendous distinction between mortal and venial sin, between eternal separation from God and the temporary loss of His favour.

Now I say that a compulsory confessional system based on such principles, or rather such absence of principle, may easily cause distress of mind when there ought to be peace and joy, or may produce the belief that we have been forgiven when there has been no true repentance at all; while in every case it puts a fearful power into the hands of a fallible priest in a matter really belonging to the transactions of the human soul with a Merciful Father, through a sufficient Saviour, in the strength of the Holy Ghost.

I will conclude what I have to say under

* To the fifth and tenth of Pascal's famous Provincial Letters, which exposed the immoral consequence of the Jesuit doctrine of Probabilities, should now be added the sixth chapter of Professor Huber's recent "Order of the Jesuits" (Berlin, 1873).

this head with four remarks, which are partially repetitions of what has been said before, but which have the advantage of being very definite.

First, let it be remembered that the decision of the confessor in regard to these delicate and difficult affairs of the soul is *judicial*. Under this system the voice of God within the Church is not the Holy Ghost, freely instructing and training the conscience of each separate person according to the diligent use which is made of prayer and other means of obtaining light; but it is found in the precarious utterances of a caste of men set apart from their fellows, yet without having a perfect knowledge of the awful secrets with which they have to deal.

Next, it is obvious that this system creates a necessity for *a minute casuistical training*. Such training must, in fact, preponderate over everything else; and thus the proportions of a well-balanced theology must inevitably be disturbed. It is probable that within the Church of England inadequate attention is given to the study of cases of conscience; and that in this respect we suffer, and have some new and very useful lessons to learn. But excess of this study is far more harmful than the lack of it. Few things can be more injurious than the overshadowing of the Bible by a thick network of artificial divinity. I well remember the earnestness with which in Italy, a few years ago, a professor in a theological seminary told me privately of his craving for a method of Biblical training instead of the scholastic and casuistical method which was there supreme: but then, he added, he was, so far as he knew, alone in having these thoughts; and if he revealed them, he would be a marked and ruined man.

Again, it seems evident that when the Clergy of a country are trained under this system, there must grow up among the people what may be called a *quantitative* morality— a morality not of principle and feeling, but of less or more, and of nice rules and distinctions, and that thus the general tone of

Christian sentiment must be lowered. The adoption, too, of the doctrine of probabilities as a theory, among the guides of the people, must necessarily have its counterpart among the people themselves in a habit of acting on probabilities. It need not be doubted, indeed, that when the confessor is saintly and the penitent is earnest, a high spirit of devotion may be generated under the practice of Sacramental Confession. But can the average conscience fail to be injured, when the standard books of morality direct attention, with the most minute ingenuity, to the qualifications and reservations and excuses which modify the character of sin?

To conclude, this aspect of the subject is very serious for us at this time; for Roman Catholic teaching on morals is sure to have influence amongst us, in proportion as the practice of auricular confession spreads; and Roman Catholic teaching on morals is now *Jesuit* teaching. The genius of Pascal has been in vain. Within a very few years we hear that the text-books in nearly all Roman

Catholic countries have been changed. The clerical seminaries are now pervaded by that which Pascal opposed. The Jesuits have been well described as being now "the Church of Rome in commission." It is not a light thing that the confessional is exposing us to the danger of acquiring, in reference to matters of right and wrong, habits of thought inspired by that celebrated Order.

CHAPTER IV.

THE BIBLE: CONFESSION TO MAN.

WHEN the relation of Sacramental Confession to the Holy Scriptures is set down as the question to be considered, the mind turns immediately and instinctively to that familiar verse in the Epistle of St. James —"*Confess* your faults one to another, and pray one for another, that ye may be healed: the effectual fervent prayer of a righteous man availeth much."*

Confession is here enjoined, or, at least, very strongly recommended. But what kind of confession? Not confession to a priest, for the sake of obtaining absolution; but mutual

* James v. 16.

confession, that there may be the benefit of mutual help, and that each may pray for the other.

And the case is made stronger by the fact that in the preceding verses the Elders of the Church, or the Presbyters—or the Priests, if we prefer to use the Saxon abbreviation of the Greek word *—are very distinctly mentioned. St. James has been speaking of them, and now he turns from them to the relations of ordinary Christians one among another. In reading through the fifteenth and sixteenth verses consecutively, we observe a marked transition; and in the sixteenth verse the writer has passed over his line of demarcation from one subject to another. This transition gives all the greater emphasis to what he says concerning reciprocal confession and reciprocal intercession.

Yet, strange to say, the text is confidently used to authorise the system which is termed "auricular confession," or "sacramental con-

---

* It cannot be too often repeated that "priest," to invert Milton's phrase, is merely "presbyter *writ short*."

fession," where the penitent confesses to the priest, but the priest does not confess to the penitent; where nothing mutual, nothing reciprocal takes place; where all the confession is on one side; where one person makes known the secrets of his life, and the other keeps both those communicated secrets and his own. Not long ago, for instance, I saw in a continental cathedral, in a series of pictures representing what are called the Seven Sacraments, this text appended to that which indicated the "Sacrament of Penance." Such unfair dealing with Holy Scripture suggests the feeling of *distrust;* and one of the most painful states of mind connected with this whole subject is the feeling of *distrust.*

Let us see how a Roman Catholic commentator of high repute contrives to make this passage a justification for the theory and practice of Sacramental Confession. These words of St. James constitute a terrible difficulty for Roman Catholics, and for those who take the Roman Catholic view of confession and absolution: and the difficulty

must be, by them, somehow surmounted, whether by ingenuity, or by violence. Thus the Jesuit commentator, Cornelius à Lapide, says on this passage: "*One to another* means man to man, like to like, brother to brother; as, for instance, *to a priest*, who, though superior in office, is equal in nature, and himself bound to confess to a priest."*
This (to express my own feeling honestly) I regard as merely an attempt to show that when St. James said one thing, he meant another; or, in plain English, an attempt, by throwing a haze over the whole subject, to show that black is white.

But now it is important to observe—and this circumstance may be expected to have some weight with those who are pre-disposed to accept Roman teaching upon the subject before us—that Roman Catholic writers are not unanimous in their interpretations of this passage in St. James. I turn to another commentator, also a Jesuit. I take into my

* "Comment. in Sacram. Scripturam." Par., MDCCCLX. Vol. x. p. 583.

hand Lorinus; and in his pages I find these words, "That phrase, *one to another*, does not justify the view of the heretics, or of Cajetan, and other Catholics too, who, because of it, deny that the reference in this place is to Sacramental Confession."* And who was Cajetan? He was the court theologian of Leo X. He did more than any one man of his day to move forward the doctrine of the Pope's Infallibility from its previous position of a floating opinion towards its present state of fixed dogma. He it was who, though he had seen Sixtus IV., Innocent VIII., and Alexander VI., was the author of the saying that, "The Catholic Church is the born handmaid of the Pope."† He it was that was sent to Augsburg to demand the retractation of Luther, who had dared to maintain that Indulgences, consisting of the merits of Christ and the Saints, are not at the disposal of the Pope. This Cajetan, then, this Roman of the Romans, takes the Protestant view of the

* "Comment. in Cathol. Epist." Lugd., MDCXIX. P. 293.
† See "Janus" (English Transl.), p. 375.

text before us. I feel that this is more than enough for my present purpose. With so great a champion on my side I need not refer to any others.

Observing, however, that Estius, another Roman Catholic commentator, has been referred to with singular confidence in the course of recent discussions on this subject, I cannot resist the temptation of referring to him likewise. I confess I was myself somewhat startled, when I took down his second volume from my shelf, and found that he leaves the interpretation of the passage an open question. He states that three views may be taken, either that St. James means the acknowledgment of faults to those whom we have offended, or the opening out of our sins and difficulties to a friend for the purpose of obtaining advice, or that he refers to "Sacramental Confession:" and Estius concludes, "Inasmuch as the two former meanings, especially the second, are not without probability, and inasmuch as thoroughly Catholic writers have advocated this meaning, therefore let the reader have full liberty to choose which he prefers of the two, or even of the three." * I need not say more. Roman Catholic commentators being divided, the language of St. James is left free to receive its natural interpretation.

In consequence of the obvious prominence of this passage in its bearing on the present controversy, and also of the boldness with which it has been used for a purpose to which it is clearly inapplicable, I have dwelt upon it at some length, reserving other parts of the Biblical argument for the next chapter. Nor need I hesitate to repeat here, in substance, what was said in preaching on this text. It is very important, in debates of this kind, to ascertain not only what a Scriptural text does not mean, but what it does mean. If it can be seen that the words of St. James, naturally interpreted, have a copious significance, directly available for the promotion of Christian life, the temptation to use them in another way is much diminished.

* "Comment. in Epist. Apost." Par., MDCLXVI. Vol. ii. p. 1107.

Mutual or reciprocal confession—of friends among friends—that there may be mutual and reciprocal help and mutual and reciprocal intercession, this is quite consistent with confession to Almighty God, and quite a different thing from confession to a priest, for the sake of obtaining that priest's absolution. There ought to be more of such confession amongst us than there is. An Apostle recommends it: and with good reason. There is far too little acknowledgment of our faults to one another. We are far too proud, far too reserved, too unwilling to be blamed, too ready to justify ourselves: and thus we lose much help that would be invaluable for the progress of the Christian life.

First, when we have done any wrong to others, have erred in temper, have dealt unfairly, have yielded to selfishness, there ought to be a free and cheerful acknowledgment. If our Lord says, "Tell thy brother *his* fault between thee and him alone,"* surely

* Matt. xviii. 15.

He would approve of our saying, "Tell him *thy* fault between him and thee alone." This is a kind of auricular confession which is thoroughly wholesome, thoroughly good.

Next, in our more public relations, we ought to be willing to make a frank acknowledgment, when we are aware that we have been wrong. In the case of such discussions as these, for instance, a mistake should be admitted, if a mistake has been made. Nothing is lost by this course. In most cases, probably other men see very plainly that we have been wrong; and we only make matters worse by pretending that we have been right. By confession we shall gain something in general esteem. A man who can make an acknowledgment of error is almost always respected. No one is surprised that we should fall into error: no one expects that we should always be right; and the world is commonly generous, if by confession we do all that can be done to remedy our mistake.

Above all, there should be confidential

confession (with due discretion, of course) of Christian friends among Christian friends. By the mere fact that such persons are Christ's true disciples, they are made to help one another. Let faults and weaknesses and follies be admitted. Let advice be sought. Let sympathy have its appointed and most blessed work. So will oil and wine be poured into many a sore and festering wound. So will feeble resolutions be invigorated. So will the straight road to Heaven be resumed with gladness of heart.

And, finally, this mutual help must especially take the form of *prayer*. The help that is really given must come from God. "Pray for one another, that ye may be healed," is the second part, and not less important part, of this apostolic precept. And we are called upon most carefully to observe how St. James concludes. His closing words rivet and fasten down immovably the true meaning of the passage: "The effectual fervent prayer of a righteous man availeth much." He does not say, "The absolution of a priest availeth much." If he had meant this, he would have said this. In a matter so important, it is incredible that he could have led us wrong. We must at least believe that St. James knew the use of words; or rather we ought to say, we are sure that the Holy Ghost, who inspired him so to write, does not deceive us. May it ever be granted to us, in these sad and disturbing times, to prefer "the words which," in the Scriptures of truth, "the Holy Ghost teacheth," to "the words which man's wisdom teacheth,"* wherever they are found!

* 1 Cor. ii. 13.

CHAPTER V.

THE BIBLE: CONFESSION TO GOD.

THE relation of our subject to Holy Scripture is of such paramount importance, that two chapters of this small volume are not too much to give to it; and a convenient division can be made, with the Bible before us, between Confession to Man and Confession to God.

I will not dwell here on the relation which subsists between the teaching of the Bible and the teaching of the Church, or on the limitation which we ought to give to the meaning of the word "Church." This, on the present occasion, may justly be treated as a collateral topic; for in the recent discussions on "Sacramental Confession" which have come before my notice, the Scriptures have been referred to, on both sides, and on all sides, boldly, freely, and directly. Some who have written on the subject evidently view the voice of Scripture as subordinate to the voice of the Church; others regard it as giving the knowledge of our Religion in a far clearer and more authentic form than any, which is found elsewhere. But in dealing with this question we should really be considering the ground for being Christians at all, rather than the matter which is actually before us. I will not then attempt to decide between those who, in the exercise of their private judgment, accept Holy Scripture as sufficiently containing a Divine Revelation, and, in the exercise of that judgment, reverently use all helps supplied by Christian antiquity and Christian experience for interpreting Holy Scripture; and those, on the other hand, who, in the exercise of their private judgment, accept the Church as their one authoritative teacher, and who, in the further exercise of that judgment, have decided (since July 18th, 1870) that the Pope is the Church. Those who have written on the Roman Catholic side having appealed to the Bible freely and unreservedly, I will do the same.

Enough has been said concerning that passage in the Epistle of St. James, where he urges the benefit of mutual acknowledgment of faults, and the benefit of mutual help through intercessory prayer. No advantage could be gained by further observations on a text which, when looked at with simplicity, stands out so clearly and definitely in its natural meaning. Several other passages, however, of Scripture have been adduced in the course of this controversy; some having a serious bearing on the matter in hand, others so irrelevant, that it is difficult to avoid a smile, when they are brought forward in this connection. Of the second class are quotations from the Old Testament, which sometimes surprise us by their appearance in this connection. Thus, for instance, it is startling to find the public confession of Achan before all the people of Israel brought forward as an argument for *another* kind of Confession, the great characteristic of which is that it is secret.* Of similar value is a reference to that passage in the Book of Proverbs, where we are told that "he that covereth his sins shall not prosper, but whoso *confesseth* and forsaketh them shall find mercy;" † as though confession to God in Jewish times could possibly be a precedent for compulsory confession to a priest in Christian times. Still, the Old Testament has its instructive lessons for us in reference to the subject—but for this reason, that this part of the Bible is replete with injunctions that we *should confess to God*, while nothing whatever is found there to enjoin the seeking of *private absolution from man.*

* "Joshua said unto Achan, My son, give, I pray thee, glory to the Lord God of Israel, and *make confession* unto Him; and tell me now what thou hast done; hide it not from me." Josh. vii. 19. With this public confession to God in the time of Joshua, compare similar instances in the times of Hezekiah and Ezra. 2 Chron. xxx. 22, Ezra x. 11.

† Prov. xxviii. 13. See Ps. xxxii. 5, Dan. ix. 4.

But I turn to the New Testament, and I am met by an argument for Sacramental Confession based on the words of St. Matthew, in which he states that, during the preaching of John the Baptist, "Jerusalem, and all Judæa, and all the region round about Jordan, went out to him, and were baptized of him in Jordan, *confessing* their sins." * In this argument St. John the Baptist is represented as receiving into his ear the private confessions of all these people, and giving them private absolution. I find it difficult to comprehend how any one could present this supposition, except with a desire to introduce the element of laughter into a very serious subject. I do not doubt, however, that some who reason thus are quite in earnest. Let us then look at the matter gravely. The chief stress of the Roman Catholic case is laid upon the words of our Saviour on the evening after His resurrection,† and presumed to be addressed to the Apostles and their successors. But these words had not been spoken in the days of

* Matt. iii. 5, 6.   † John xx. 23.

John the Baptist. How then could he exercise a responsibility arising out of these subsequent words? He was not a successor of the Apostles, but a predecessor. He was great indeed as a prophet; none before him ever greater; but we are told by an infallible Speaker that " he that is least in the kingdom of God is greater " than the Baptist.* On the Roman Catholic view of the authority for sacramental binding and loosing, John the Baptist, in exercising this function, would have been an usurper; and yet he is quoted by Roman Catholics in illustration and in defence of Sacramental Confession. Usurpation is brought forward to illustrate and to justify legal authority. But still, let me add, in this case, as above, when reference was made to the Old Testament, the work and the words of John the Baptist have an important bearing upon the subject before us. He did not sit as " a judge " in the private confessional; but he openly pointed to " the Lamb of God, which taketh away the sin of the

* Luke vii. 28.

world;"* and this is precisely what was done by St. Peter, when he preached to the Jews at Pentecost, and by St. Paul when he wrote to his Heathen converts. The teaching and conduct of the Baptist, in regard to this matter, is in strict harmony with the general analogy of the Bible.

A second passage in the New Testament, the quoting of which in this connection is almost equally startling, has reference to the experience of this last Apostle at Ephesus. A great commotion took place there in consequence of his preaching and of the miracles he was enabled to work. "Many that believed came and *confessed*, and showed their deeds," and magical books were publicly burnt.† This, too, is adduced as a proof that private compulsory Sacramental Confession was an Apostolic institution. There is, however, in two respects, the most glaring contradiction between the two cases. The confession of evil deeds—if, indeed, it was not rather *the confession of Christ*, which is

* John i. 29, 36.   † Acts xix. 18, 19.

elsewhere denoted by the same Greek word *—was, first, *spontaneous and voluntary*, and, secondly, *public and open*. In preaching the first of my sermons on the general subject in Chester, I said that no one would dare to bring forward this passage in justification of imperative auricular confession; but I have found myself obliged to alter the sentence in which I said this. All that need be added on this point is, that if this passage is to be pressed into the service of the present question at all, it is a very strong argument for the public acknowledgment of sin, and public humiliation for sin, and, therefore, a very strong argument against the secret confessional.

But there remains a passage of serious and solemn import, made more serious and solemn by the occasion and the time, when the words recorded by St. John were spoken.† It was the evening of the first Easter Day All being now accomplished that was necessary for our Redemption,— Christ, "having

* Phil. ii. 11. † John xx. 21—23.

THE BIBLE : CONFESSION TO GOD.   61

died for our sins and risen for our justification," proceeded to found that society which was to bear His name, and to continue through the ages till He should come again. Speaking to His assembled Church, to the Apostles and Disciples—*not to the Apostles alone*, as we see from St. Luke *—and using a form of words familiar to the members of Jewish Synagogues,† though now with a far higher than any merely Jewish meaning, He invested His Church with the loftiest powers that can belong to a religious society on earth, and promised His ratification to

---

* When the two disciples returned from Emmaus, they found not only "the eleven gathered together," but "them that were with them." Luke xxiv. 33. See ver. 36.

† See "Excursus on the Power of the Keys," appended to Professor Plumptre's recent University Sermon on "Confession and Absolution," especially as regards Matt. xvi. 19 and xviii. 18. I cannot indeed agree in the view which limits the application of John xx. 23 to cases where a special prophetic insight enables men to read the heart. The remark, however, is important (Sermon, p. 32), that it is to the *prophet*, rather than to the *priest*, that the office belongs of saying, on the one hand, "The Lord hath put away thy sin," as in 2 Sam. xii. 13, and on the other, "Thou hast rejected the word of the Lord, and the Lord hath rejected thee," as in 1 Sam. xv. 26.

the exercise of those powers. To the grave and reverential consideration of this passage I shall return in a later chapter, having reference to the position of the Church of England in regard to this subject. At present all I will say is this, that Christ founded not only a new religion, but a new society, and that all the ordinances and regulations of this society have reference to the salvation of the soul. We should expect then His words on such an occasion to be solemn and comprehensive. Let us add together the admission of converts into the Church by Holy Baptism; the preaching* of a

---

* The solemn and sufficient meaning of these words, *if limited only to preaching*, was forcibly urged by the present Dean of Manchester in a recent ordination sermon. "I believe myself that these words meant to convey the power to preach the Gospel, to announce to men *salvation* from sin, which, if neglected, would infallibly lead to *destruction*—that these men, St. Peter, the Apostles, and the body of faithful disciples, had entrusted to them a Gospel, or Divine message, from Heaven, which, if accepted, would lead to life, if neglected, would leave men in condemnation; and, therefore, that they imply the overwhelming importance of the Truth, to which they were ordained to bear testimony, and the Authority by which they acted." The work of the Apostles, he adds, was "to call men into the new covenant of

Gospel, which to some is "a savour of life unto life," to others "a savour of death unto death;" the reception of Christians to the Holy Communion, or the debarring of them from this sacrament; and the exercise of discipline, which must vary in detail at different periods; and we shall not find it difficult to assign to our Saviour's words an ample and awful meaning, with a continuous application to the Church in every age. Only, this must be remembered—that there is not one single syllable in the passage to sanction the belief that the office of Christ's Ministers was to be "judicial," that they were to divide sins into "mortal" and "venial," and that they were to require the "auricular" confession of the former in order to forgiveness.

But collateral arguments from Scripture also have been employed: and I quite admit the force of such collateral arguments, if they are

---

regeneration: those who obeyed received new life; those who disobeyed remained under the wrath of God." I quote from the *Manchester Courier* of March 10th, 1873.

consistent with themselves, and if they bring forth the meaning of obscure texts through combination with others that are more clear.* I, too, will use a collateral argument: and it is this: That nowhere in the New Testament is there a trace that the words spoken by our Lord on the evening of the first Easter Day were understood by the Apostles to mean what Roman Catholics suppose them to mean

---

* I have seen, for instance, a justification of Sacramental Confession drawn from the mysterious notice of Melchizedek in the Bible. The argument, if I rightly apprehend it, stands thus: Christ is "a priest for ever, after the order of Melchizedek." Christ says, in the passage quoted from St. John's Gospel, "As my Father sent me, even so send I you:" the words thus addressed to that assembly are also addressed to the successors of the Apostles: therefore, the Clergy now are priests like Melchizedek. But there is no evidence that Melchizedek was appointed to receive private confessions and give private absolution. This act, too, of absolving is not a priestly but a judicial act, and is so set forth in the Canons of the Council of Trent. Moreover, the argument proves too much. Melchizedek was a king as well as a priest, and certainly our Lord is King. Hence the Clergy are kings as well as priests. And indeed St. Peter, whom Roman Catholics must recognise as the greatest of the Popes, does put these two thoughts together, applying them both to the Christian Church, when he says, "Ye are a royal priesthood." But then he assigns this double designation to all Christians, Clergy and Laity alike.

now. The Pastoral Epistles relate specially to the office of the Clergy, and we find no such indication there: the Acts of the Apostles give an account of the early founding of the Church, and there, too, we search in vain for anything of the kind; and the same thing is true of the letters of the Apostles, whether they be St. Peter or St. Paul, St. John or St. James. Everything in the New Testament, in reference to this matter, shows consistency; but this consistency is absolutely opposed to Vatican or semi-Vatican Christianity.

And I will go one step further. There are several passages in the New Testament, where an allusion to Sacramental Confession must have occurred, if Vatican or semi-Vatican Christianity were the true expression of the Gospel of Christ. Thus: "If any man lack wisdom"—would not, on this hypothesis, the sentence have most naturally ended by advice to have recourse to a confessor or director? Again, when St. Paul says, of preparation for the Lord's Supper, "Let a man examine himself, and so let him eat of that bread, and drink of that cup," is it credible, if the necessity of privately confessing to a priest were a Divinely-instituted law, that all reference to this solemn fact should be omitted? Can we even read without perplexity our Blessed Lord's own words—"Come unto me, all ye that labour and are heavy-laden"— if He Himself intended that recourse to a human priest should be an essential preliminary to the obtaining of relief and rest? And what are we to say of the Parable of the Prodigal Son? Surely that prodigal had been guilty of mortal sin. Whence is it that the father *anticipates* his return, and welcomes him without any one to intervene? Surely the parable would have been more natural and complete, on the Roman hypothesis, and less likely to deceive us, if the younger brother had been represented as first visiting the elder brother in the confessional. But I will not proceed in the enumeration of instances. I will suggest that any one who has doubts on this subject should read the New Testament carefully, with this one thought in his mind, and should *pause*, whenever he comes to a passage where he would *expect* some allusion to Sacramental Confession to occur, on the supposition of its being an essential part of the Gospel. It will strike him as remarkable that a system, asserted to be of Divine institution, should have been unknown to the Apostles; and his natural conclusion will be that this system was the product of a later age. To this aspect of our subject we shall come in the next chapter, where it will be considered in connection with Church History.

CHAPTER VI.

CHURCH HISTORY.

IN the second part of the threefold sentence which I have quoted, as a kind of text, from Bishop Blomfield's Charge of 1842, it is said that this system of compulsory auricular confession is "one of the worst corruptions of the Church of Rome." By the word "corruption" we mean that the thing to which it is applied has been, more or less, vitiated, depraved, debased; so that, while originally it may have been very good, it is now very bad. Thus, in speaking of this system in the Church of Rome as a corruption, we view it as a spoiling of that which was primitive.

The most primitive Church of all, in reference to this matter, has already been considered in the chapters on the Bible. We must now think of the primitive Church in another and secondary sense. Faithful members of our communion are always in the habit of referring cheerfully and confidently to the few first centuries of the Christian era, not as overruling the Scripture, not as being exempt from the germs of a gradually-spreading corruption, but as collaterally justifying our interpretation of Scripture, and as adding great strength to our religious position. In the present instance there need be no hesitation in the cheerful confidence of this appeal to the early ages.

In moving up towards these ages it is well to secure some definite starting-points. When we view the subject before us historically, our attention ought to be fixed very closely and carefully on the Fourth Lateran Council, when, in 1215, private confession to a priest was first made imperative, and on the Council of Trent, when, in 1551, the theory and practice of such Auricular Confession were dogmatically defined and prescribed. It is of the utmost importance, in this controversy, to observe the *general characteristics* of these two ecclesiastical epochs. I will begin with the later of the two, and thence move upwards in the direction of the primitive times.

The Council of Trent was, if I may use such a comparison, the watershed of all Modern Church History. The Roman Catholic religion, in some of its essential principles, was then first defined. Doctrines, which may be said to have previously been in a fluid state, were then crystallized. The Roman Church then separated itself both from the whole Protestant world, and from Oriental Christianity, while yet in this very act of separation it declared itself universal. With the definition, too, of doctrine came the consolidation of practice. The hierarchy was more strongly organized: discipline was tightened: seminaries were established for the training of the Clergy in strict principles; and the Papal power came out from the conflicts of this Council, far greater than it had been in the previous century. It is essential to take into account all these things, when we wish to obtain a just view of Sacramental Confession, as it emerged from the hands of Pope Pius IV. That which had been made a rule in the thirteenth century was now formulated in systematic and authoritative teaching. A corrupt practice was now developed into organized error and mischief. To the ripe fruit of this Roman Confessional System some reference will be made in the concluding chapter of this little volume. I will only add here, in regard to the topic immediately before us, that the records of the discussion which took place at the Council of Trent, indicate very clearly two currents of opinion, with various subordinate streams on either side, struggling for the mastery.* At length the definitions concerning Sacramental Confession came forth in the form which was the natural result of the decree of 1215, after the opportunity

* See Paolo Sarpi's "Historie of the Councell of Trent" (Brent's Translation, 1620), book iv. pp. 345-359.

given by three centuries and a half for the development of its legitimate effects.

Turning now to the decree of the Fourth Lateran Council, again we are bound attentively to consider the circumstances which were associated with it. Only thus are we able to see its true and full significance. The very name of Innocent III. shows that the change in question must have been *an advance* in the power of the hierarchy. Let it be remembered, too, that at this time first the word "transubstantiation—" itself an assertion of the highest sacerdotal prerogative —began to be authoritatively used: let it be remembered again that in this Council the power of deposing a Sovereign Prince was assumed by the Church, and that this epoch "bequeathed to the Papacy its two great standing armies," the Franciscans and Dominicans;* and it will easily be seen that the

---

* Dean Milman's "History of Latin Christianity," vol. vi. p. 50. It should not be overlooked that a still more efficient "standing army" of the Papacy was recruited at the later of the two great dates to which reference is here made.

decree concerning Confession was no isolated fact, but a part of a vast progress made at that time in priestly usurpation. As regards the decree itself, the obvious remark is suggested, that if it made Auricular Confession compulsory, such confession cannot have been compulsory before. Hence the statement of the Canons of the Council of Trent, that the system as *then* observed had been established at the beginning of Christianity, must be erroneous. In fact Pope Innocent III. seems to me to have refuted by anticipation Pope Pius IV.]

Not that this was really the beginning of the observance of Sacramental Confession. Some Protestants have written and spoken on this subject in a wild and random way, and have thus done harm to the cause they have desired to help. A great ecclesiastical change like that of 1215 does not come without previous preparation. The recent declaration of the Pope's Infallibility, to adduce a similar instance, was prepared for by the growth of opinion, by systematic teaching in Clerical Seminaries, by the alteration of Catechisms,* and by the influence of the Order of the Jesuits. So in an earlier period the assertion of sacerdotal power by the Clergy, the claim to supremacy on the part of the Popes, the general ignorance which promoted superstition, and the natural craving for an absolution which was believed to be efficacious, paved the way for a system which had been unknown to primitive times. Auricular Confession, *once admitted to be desirable*, prevailed more and more, and that which had been voluntary tended more and more to become compulsory.† It is precisely this historical train of circumstances, this easy succession of cause and effect, which

---

* Some very remarkable evidence on this subject is furnished by the Abbé Michaud, in his treatise " De la Falsification des Catéchismes Français et des Manuels de Théologie par le parti Romaniste de 1670 à 1868 " (Paris, 1872).

† During the season of Lent last year, in the course of a catechetical instruction to about fifty young women and three or four young men, an English Clergyman appealed to them very earnestly thus, " Suppose you were to die before Easter without having confessed ! " If confession to a priest is of such value to the soul, is it not a mercy to make it compulsory ?

fills many thoughtful persons with anxiety now in England, where ominous symptoms of a *preparatory* kind are plainly to be seen.

As to citations from the Fathers on the subject of Auricular Confession, it would not be difficult to make a "catena" on either side. Two long chains of contrasted authorities, in reference to this topic, might easily be hung up over against one another. It would be waste of space to fill these few pages with matter of this kind. The readers, too, of much that is written on this subject ought to be warned against second-hand quotations. I will simply adduce Chrysostom and Augustine, who are almost worth all the other Fathers put together; and from them I will pass at once to an immediate successor of the Apostles.

St. Chrysostom ought to have peculiar weight with us, because of a scandal which occurred in connection with the private confessional during his predecessor's time at Constantinople, and which resulted in discouragement of the auricular system.* In harmony with this state of things we find him writing thus, in his Homilies on the Epistle to the Hebrews: "Let us persuade ourselves that we have sinned; but let us say this, not in word only, but in our inmost thoughts. Let us not simply call ourselves sinners, but let us count up our sins, reckoning them according to their kinds. I say not unto thee that thou shouldst accuse thyself to other men; but I advise thee to follow the prophet's counsel, and to make thy way known to the Lord: in God's presence confess thyself: confess thyself unto the Judge."† And other

---

* The original authorities for this affair, which occupied the anxious attention of Nectarius, are Sozomen (vii. 16) and Socrates (v. 19). It seems doubtful whether this case of confession in the time of Nectarius can strictly be called auricular. Ed. Vales, (Par., 1668), pp. 279, 727.

† "Sancti Chrysostomi Opera." Ed. Savil., 1612. Vol. iv. p. 589. The "judge" here is not the priest, but Almighty God. In a similar passage, adduced by Daillé, where the penitent is advised to "show his wound to the physician, no one else being present," the "physician" is not the priest, but God, "who knows all our sins before they are committed." Dallæus "De Sacramentali sive auriculari Latinorum Confessione Disputatio" (Genev., 1661), p. 151. In another part of this com-

passages, even stronger, could be quoted to the same effect from Chrysostom. Coupling such words with the above-mentioned facts, we are necessarily brought to the conclusion that Compulsory Auricular Confession was not then viewed at Constantinople as a part of the Christian system.

Turning now from the East to the West, from the Greek of Chrysostom to the Latin of Augustine, I will refer to the celebrated "Confessions" of the latter writer. There, at the beginning of the tenth book, we find St. Augustine saying: "God knows all, whether I confess or not. What have I to do with men, that they should hear my confessions, as if they could heal my diseases— men, too, who are inquisitive into the lives of others, but idle in correcting their own? Why do they seek to learn from me what I am, who will not learn from Thee, O God,

prehensive work many quotations from Chrysostom are given. Some may be conveniently read in Bingham's "Antiquities of the Christian Church," bk. xviii. ch. 3 (Straker's Ed. vol. vi.); see also Hooker's "Ecclesiastical Polity" (Keble's Ed.), vol. iii. p. 54.

what they themselves are? Let me confess what I know concerning myself: let me confess also that which I do not know. For what I know, I know by the shining of Thy light upon me—and what I know not, I know not because my darkness, as yet, is not turned by Thy light into the noonday."* Now I venture to assert that such words could not have been written by St. Augustine, if all in his day were required to confess privately to a priest. How many Roman Catholic priests would dare to publish such words now, and to adopt them as their own?

The only other quotation I shall adduce is from Clemens Romanus, whose words ought to have great weight with us for a different reason from that which gives weight to Chrysostom and Augustine. If the Bishops of Constantinople and Hippo were men of commanding greatness, Clement lived at the very threshold of the Apostolic age. Quoting from an edition of the Earliest Fathers,

* "Sancti Augustini Opera." Ed. Benedict. Paris, 1689. Vol. i. 171, 173.

published by an eminent and learned German prelate, who, after opposing the Pope's Infallibility, now seems to have acquiesced in the Vatican decree, without having refuted his own arguments, I ask the reader's attention to the following short extract from Clement's First Epistle to the Corinthians: "It is better that a man should confess his sins than that his heart should be hardened. . . . . . My brethren, God requires nothing from us except to confess to Him."* Such is the view of the Confessional presented to us, while the stream of Divine truth flowed fresh, and as yet uncontaminated with any large admixture of human error. St. Clement seems to have known as little as the Apostles themselves of any sacramental and imperative system of private confession.

These are very scanty specimens of a mass of early Christian literature, which might be

* "Pat. Apostolici." Ed. Hefele, p. 127. The passage will be found in Bishop Jacobson's Edition, vol. i. pp. 186-188. It should be added, in justice to Bishop Hefele, that, like Strossmayer, he does not appear to have yet published the Vatican decree officially in his diocese.

brought forward in illustration of the point before us: but, for the reasons above given, these particular quotations have peculiar force. It is not overlooked that besides extracts from the writings of the Fathers, elucidations of our subject are to be obtained from liturgical materials. A fit place, however, for a reference to such sources will be found in a chapter relating to Ordination and Absolution; and the same opportunity will be convenient for some reference to that ancient penitential system, of which the modern Confessional is the "corruption."*

* The transmutation of the public discipline of the Early Church into the auricular confessional of the Modern Church of Rome is one of the most curious and most instructive changes which Ecclesiastical History records. For details see the second and third chapters of Marshall's "Penitential Discipline of the Primitive Church for the first 400 years after Christ, together with its Declension from the fifth century downwards to its present state." (Oxford Anglo-Catholic Library, 1844.)

CHAPTER VII.

THE CHURCH OF ENGLAND.

WE come now to the consideration of the doctrine of the Church of England in respect of Confession and Absolution. Our authorities must, of course, be the Thirty-nine Articles, and the various services and rubrics of the Prayer-Book.

And here a general remark, which, though negative, is really of the utmost importance, must be made at the outset. The entire absence from any part of these Articles and this Book of any of that instruction concerning Sacramental Confession, which forms a most conspicuous feature of the utterances of the Council of Trent, shows that, in this matter, there is a gulf between the Churches of England and Rome. Even at first sight it is evident that this gulf is too broad to be logically bridged over. But let us turn to some particulars, which can be examined separately.

Our Twenty-fifth Article states that Penance is not "a Sacrament of the Gospel," that it has not "the like nature of a Sacrament" with Baptism and the Lord's Supper. Those then who advocate and urge on, within our Church, the practice of *Sacramental* Confession—which, as we have seen, means Confession viewed as an essential part of *the Sacrament of Penance*—when that Church has asserted that Penance is not a Christian Sacrament at all, would startle us extremely, if the startling theological effects of the day had not somewhat blunted our sense of wonder.

But the Articles deal with this matter indirectly as well as directly. In the Thirty-fifth of them the Homilies are referred to with more than approbation: and in one of these old-fashioned sermons the subject of Confession and Absolution is prominent. No one supposes that every phrase in the Homilies is to be quoted as of authority. It is their broad and general teaching which the Church of England accepts and inculcates : but that the acceptance and inculcation of this broad and general teaching ought to be a reality seems evident from the reference made to the Homilies in the rubric which follows the Nicene Creed in our Communion Service.* And here I cannot help referring with pain to the fact, that in a most important communication on the subject before us, made public a few months ago, an *incidental* expression was quoted from the Homilies, as being in the interest of Sacramental Confession, and as giving the sanction of our Church for the practice, whereas no notice was taken of their *explicit, distinct,* and *direct* declaration *against* such Confession. This manner of citing authorities seems hardly worthy of the candour that might be expected from learned

* See also Art. xi.

divines, such as are some of those who attached their names to the document in question.*

The words of the Homily on "Repentance," which refer to this subject, have often been quoted: but, as there seems to be a disposition in some minds to put these words out of sight, it is desirable to quote them here again; and no commentary on them need be added. "Whereas the adversaries go about to wrest this place † for to maintain their auricular confession withal, they are greatly deceived themselves, and do shamefully deceive others: for if this text ought to be understood of auricular confession, then the priests are as much bound to confess themselves unto the lay-people, as the lay-people are bound to confess themselves to them. And if to

---

* I refer to the "Declaration," which, after appearing in the "Times," was afterwards printed in the "Guardian" of December 10th, 1873. The serious nature of this document cannot be questioned. It bears the signatures, not only of the Principal of a Theological College, but of three Divinity Professors in one of our Universities, and among them the Professor of Pastoral Theology.

† *Viz.*, James v. 16.

pray is to absolve, then the laity by this place hath as great authority to absolve the priests as the priests have to absolve the laity." A later passage in the same Homily is as follows: "I do not say, but that, if any do find themselves troubled in conscience, they may repair to their learned curate or pastor, or to some other godly learned man, and show the trouble and doubt of their conscience to them, that they may receive at their hand the comfortable salve of God's Word; but it is against the true Christian liberty that any man should be bound to the numbering of his sins, as it hath been used heretofore in the time of his blindness and ignorance."* This language is strictly in harmony with what we

---

* It is evidently right that this contemporary language should be put side by side with that Warning in our Communion Service, which is commented on below. We remark too that it tends rather to dilute than to intensify the expressions in that Warning. Thus, "the comfortable salve of God's Word" seems synonymous with "comfort and the benefit of absolution"; and here it is suggested to those who are troubled in conscience that they may repair, not necessarily to "some discreet and learned *minister*," but to some "godly learned *man*."

find in the rubrics and services of the Prayer-Book, to which we may now turn.

In examining the English Book of Common Prayer there are three dates, to which every intelligent student of English Church-history gives his careful attention. These dates are 1549, 1552, and 1662. Very marked changes took place in the book between the two former of these years. It would not, however, be quite fair to pause, in arguments of this kind, at the second of these years, as, though we obtained then the full and final expression of the mind of the English Church, after that date a reaction, to a limited extent, set in: so that it is essential to consider not only what was removed or changed in 1552, but whether anything so removed or changed was replaced or modified in 1662. A good illustration of this point is furnished by the liturgical history of the word "Altar," which appears several times in the Prayer-Book of 1549, but which was everywhere removed at the second date, and nowhere replaced at the third—the phrase "Table," or "Lord's Table," or "Holy Table," being substituted, and everywhere remaining.* Nothing can be more emphatic than this deliberate and repeated testimony to the rejection of the doctrine of a sacrificial priesthood. So with the withdrawal and non-restitution of expressions which might be held to favour the theory and practice of Sacramental Confession. This can be shown very clearly under two heads: the first having reference to the Warning appointed to be read before the administration of the Holy Communion, the second to the form of Private Absolution provided in 1549 for cases of Private Confession.

Let us compare the Warning, as it stood in

* Nothing seems more strange than the attempt to meet this argument by a reference to the use of the word " Altar " in the Coronation Service. Even if a single exception had remained, when the utmost pains had been taken to remove every trace of this significant word, such an exception would have been of no great weight against overwhelming evidence. But, further, the Coronation Service is no part of the Prayer-Book at all: it never received the sanction of Convocation; and an Erastian argument is of very little force, when used by those who vehemently condemn Erastianism.

that year, and as it stood in 1552 and 1662, and still stands. In the first instance we read thus:—" If there be any of you, whose conscience is troubled and grieved in anything lacking comfort or counsel, let him come to me, or to some other discreet and learned priest taught in the law of God, and confess and open his sin and grief secretly, that he may receive such ghostly counsel, advice, and comfort, that his conscience may be relieved, and that of us, as of the Ministers of God and of the Church, he may receive comfort and absolution, to the satisfaction of his mind and avoiding of all scruple and doubtfulness." And then follows an injunction that those, on the one hand, who are "satisfied with a general confession," are not to be "offended with them that do use, to their further satisfying, the auricular and secret confession to a priest;" nor those, on the other hand, "which think it needful or convenient, for the quietness of their own consciences, particularly to open their sin to the priest, to be offended with them that are satisfied with their humble confession to God and the general confession to the Church." Now all this indicates very clearly a period of transition. The question is: In what direction did the stream begin to run from this point, and in what direction is it running still? And the answer to this question is not difficult.

In the first place all allusion to "auricular" confession, as a permissible and probable alternative along with "general" confession, is entirely omitted from the latter part of this Warning; and we never afterwards find anything of the kind restored to the Prayer-Book. Such an absolute banishment of a most significant sentence is surely of some weight for those who are disposed to be convinced. As to the earlier part of the Warning, we know that it is read now as follows: "Because it is requisite that no man should come to the Holy Communion but with a full trust in God's mercy, and with a quiet conscience, therefore, if there be any of you who by this means cannot quiet his own conscience herein, but requireth further comfort or counsel, let him come to me, or to some other discreet and learned Minister of God's Word, and open his grief—that by the Ministry of God's Holy Word he may receive the benefit of absolution, to the quieting of his conscience and avoiding of all scruple and doubtfulness." Even on a careless reading we are conscious of the great alteration which has taken place in the whole tone and tenor of the passage. But when we look into it closely, we become aware of the extreme pains which must have been taken so to alter the phraseology, that it should give no countenance whatever to that system of Sacramental Confession, which was about that time receiving its mature form at the hands of the Council of Trent. We mark especially the six following verbal changes —the word "confess" in relation to private intercourse with the priest is omitted, the word "secretly" is omitted, the phrase which describes "the particular opening of sin' is omitted, and not one of these expressions has been restored; and, further, instead of "priest" we now read "minister of God's Word;" instead of "the opening of sin and grief," we now read "the opening of grief;" and, above all, we observe this most important addition, that it is "the ministry of God's Word," by which comfort and the benefit of absolution are to be received.*

But, to pass now to our second head, it seems likely, from the very nature of the case, that so long as "auricular" confession was contemplated as permissible and customary for those who thought it conducive to their spiritual good, some form of private absolution would be prescribed. And this, accordingly, we discover to have been the case; for on turning to the Service for the Visitation of the Sick we find in 1549, after the form of absolution still provided there for exceptional cases, the following rubric: "The same form of absolution shall be used in all private confessions." This part of the rubric was removed between 1549 and 1552, and was

* See note above, p. 85.

never restored; nor has anything equivalent to it been reintroduced into the Prayer-Book subsequently. It is not, however, merely the fact of this removal which requires our thoughtful attention, but its removal coincidently with the above-mentioned change in the Warning, which withdraws all sanction for the practice of Sacramental Confession. If I may refer a second time to the document which has recently been submitted, in so marked a way, to public attention, I will here express the surprise and regret caused by the argument there used, that, Private Confession being free in the Church of England to all who desire it, some special form of Private Absolution is requisite and sanctioned. Such Private Confession was once encouraged, and then there was an authorised form of Private Absolution; but this encouragement and this authorisation were withdrawn simultaneously, and neither has since been restored. And yet these most significant changes are treated, in the document in question, as if they had never taken place.

On the whole it seems to me clear, from what has been written above, that the Church of England has decisively removed Private Confession from its old sacramental position —that the services and rubrics in the Prayer-Book are in harmony with the statement in the Church Catechism, that Christ has "ordained in His Church two Sacraments only, as generally necessary to salvation"— and that any private absolution by an English Clergyman is to be viewed, not as a judicial act, but as the application of the Divine Word to the special requirements of an individual soul.

Two very important passages, however, in the Prayer-Book still remain for consideration; one in that Service for the Visitation of the Sick which has just been mentioned, the other in the Service for the Ordaining of Priests. Some remarks on both will find a place in the next chapter, in connection with some historical notices of Ordination and Absolution. Meantime, strict attention may be invited to the general principle which ought to control all our discussions on this subject. Just as we are bound to interpret detached passages of Scripture "according to the proportion of the faith,"* so are we bound to interpret detached sentences of the Prayer-Book in harmony with the general analogy and obvious intention of the whole. In the very nature of things this must be the right principle to be kept in view. It cannot be otherwise. What is the fair way of endeavouring to ascertain the doctrine of the Church of England on such a subject as this? Clearly not by taking separate phrases out of their historical context—not by isolating them from the general spirit of the Book in which they are found, and then erecting on them a structure with building-materials procured from Roman quarries, but by embracing the aggregate of our official Church-documents in one view, by making just allowance for the conflicts through which these documents passed to their present shape, by treating the Prayer-Book as

* Rom. xii. 6.

reasonably as we should treat any other composite work, and by requiring the whole to interpret the part, and not the part to interpret the whole.

CHAPTER VIII.

ORDINATION AND ABSOLUTION.

THIS chapter is to contain some remarks on Ordination and Absolution, with special reference to the formula which our own Bishops use in ordaining Priests, and to the form of absolving, which—though under careful restrictions and avowedly for very exceptional cases—still is found in our Service for the Visitation of the Sick. In consequence both of the intrinsic importance of these topics and the multitude of historical and critical questions which immediately arise when they are touched, there is great difficulty in compressing what is written concerning them. I will, however, confine myself within the limits prescribed for this small book, taking my starting-point from the principle laid down at the end of the preceding chapter.*

Such a phrase as "I absolve thee," or "I forgive thee," clearly admits of two interpretations. It may denote a strictly judicial act, according to the spirit and doctrine of the Council of Trent; or it may mean a purely ministerial act, whereby some separate person, presumed to be penitent and believing, is assured that God's forgiving mercy is applicable to his special case. This matter may be illustrated by a passage which we find in the Second Epistle to the Corinthians, though that passage relates to a case rather of external discipline than of absolution in the deeper sense.†

We have seen that Sacramental Confession,

* *Viz.*, that the whole ought to be made to interpret the part, and not the part the whole.

† It must not be forgotten that this was a case of public, not private, absolution. Such too, was the character of those absolutions of the early Christian centuries, of which the modern sacramental system in the Church of Rome is a "corruption."

in the Roman signification of the term, was unknown to the Apostles. But in St. Paul's dealings with the Church of Corinth we are supplied with a very instructive instance of the exercise of discipline. In his First Epistle * he had directed, with the fullest weight of his apostolic authority, that a certain gross offender should be debarred from the privileges of Christian communion. In this sense the offender's sins were "retained." Since that time there had been penitence: and now the sins were "remitted:" now the moment was come for the offender's restoration to such communion; and the act of restoration is expressed thus—"To whom ye forgive any thing, I forgive also." † Now either this is judicial or it is ministerial: and on neither side of the alternative does the Roman Catholic view receive any support. If we take the former view, then it appears that the judicial function belongs to the Church, and not to the Apostle only—for St. Paul says, not merely "I forgive," but "ye forgive." Then what becomes

* 1 Cor. v. 3-5.   † 2 Cor. ii. 10.

of the theory of a separate priesthood, to whom alone the exercise of judicial powers in absolution belongs? But I contend that according to the analogy of the teaching in the whole of the New Testament, and, in harmony with the general tenor of his own language elsewhere, St. Paul would have disavowed strictly judicial functions in the affairs of the soul.

And if a similar question is asked in reference to the Prayer-Book: Have the words "I absolve thee," which we find in the Visitation Service, a ministerial sense, or a judicial sense?—then I contend that, according to the whole analogy of our official Church documents, we must decide for the former. How far it was wise in the compilers and revisers of our Book of Common Prayer to retain a phrase which is capable of two interpretations, and which might easily be so interpreted as to contradict the rest of their work, is a question into which I do not enter. Perhaps it was not then known, so well as it is known now, that the earlier forms of absolution in the West, down to the twelfth century, were precatory,* and that in the Eastern Church they are of that character still; and it is open to any English Churchman to regret that the Catholic form was not preferred to the local, the ancient to the modern. But it is perfectly evident that the modern form is not essential to a true absolution; otherwise there were no true absolutions in the Church at all during more than a thousand years. The point before us, however, is this: that the Articles and Prayer-

---

* The great work of Morinus, "De Disciplinâ in Administratione Sacramenti Pœnitentiæ" (Antv., 1862), had not then been published. He was a Roman Catholic, and a man of vast research. He says in the most explicit manner that he never saw or heard of an absolution, till the Twelfth Century, that was not precatory—"Formulam ordinariam absolutionis sive reconciliationis Pœnitentium fuisse deprecatoriam testantur *quotquot hactenus legi aut relata audivi* antiquitatis Ecclesiasticæ monumenta ad annum usque salutis ducentesimum suprà millesimum" (viii. 2). He tells us (p. 530) that about that period some proposed to add "absolvo te," to make the grace obtained by the priest's prayer more sure. By degrees it became customary to combine the two forms together. Then it began to be argued that the precatory form had nothing to do with the true and substantial absolution.

Book define the words, "I absolve thee," for us in a ministerial sense, while the Council of Trent defines them for Roman Catholics in a judicial sense.

In passing now from the question of absolution to that of ordination, it will be of advantage to us to take and examine, by the way, a specimen of the earlier forms of absolution. That which I select is the "Prayer for Penitents," in the Liturgy of St. James,[*] which is read as follows:—
"O Lord Jesus Christ, the Son of the Living God, who takest away the Sin of the World, who didst graciously remit to the two Debtors what they owed Thee, and to the woman who was a Sinner didst give the pardon of her sins, who with the forgiveness of the sins of the Paralytick didst grant him also a cure of his Disease; remit, pardon and forgive the sins committed, willingly or unwillingly, with knowledge or through ignorance, by transgression and disobedience: and whereinso-

---

[*] I quote from the edition of this Liturgy by Dr. Rattray, Bishop of Dunkeld, (1744), p. 107.

ever, as men clothed in flesh, and inhabitants of this world, or by the fraud of the Devil, they have been led astray in Word or Deed, I pray and beseech thee of thy ineffable Love to man that they may be absolved by thy Word, and released according to thy great goodness. Even so, O Lord, hear supplication for thy servants, and, as thou dost not delight in the remembrance of evil, overlook all their offence and deliver them from Eternal Punishment. For thou art He who hast enjoined us, saying, *Whatsoever ye shall loose on Earth shall be loosed in Heaven ;* thou art our God, a God who hast Power to have mercy, to save, and to forgive sins; and to Thee, with thy unoriginate Father, and life-giving Spirit, belongs Glory, now and ever, world without end. Amen." Other early forms, still more to our purpose as illustrative of the precatory character of primitive absolutions, might easily have been selected;[*] but this form is interesting, from its manner

---

[*] Several specimens are given by Goar: "Rituale Græcorum," (Par., 1647), pp. 662-674.

of quoting our Lord's words regarding the binding and remitting of sins.*

Coming now, by the most natural of all transitions, to the question of ordination, we find ourselves, when we consider our own ordaining formula, in the very same position as in reference to our (exceptional) absolving formula for penitents in sickness. The use of these particular words at ordinations is, in fact, very modern. The beginning of the direct employment of the phrase, "Receive the Holy Ghost," with the words that follow, belongs to the same general period as the beginning of the employment of the direct form, "I absolve thee." The history of these significant changes has been traced very definitely to the short period between the Master of the Sentences and the great St. Thomas of Aquinum.† Under these circumstances there is nothing at all disloyal in the preference of any English Churchman for

* The words here quoted are not from John xx. 23, but from Matt. xviii. 18. This, however, does not affect the argument.

† See Prof. Plumptre's Sermon on "Confession and Absolution," pp. 17-19.

the earlier form of ordaining over the later, for the Catholic over the local. The practical question, however, for the moment, relates to the interpretation which we in the English Church ought to give to this our comparatively modern and local formula. The true inspiration of the Church of Rome comes from that very period of the Middle Ages to which reference has just been made. That period gives to the Church of Rome its proper point of departure. But is this the case for us? That Church has a medieval form with a medieval, and more than medieval, commentary. We have the same form with a Protestant commentary. Is it not evident that our natural attitude, in regard to this matter, is quite contrary to the Roman?

But something more, and something of great importance, remains to be said in reference to our form of ordination. I firmly believe—paradoxical as this appears—that this part of the Prayer-Book is really, in its honest intention, one of the most Protestant parts of the whole volume. The Reformers found these words in customary use at ordinations. They knew that they were our Lord's own words. They dealt with them as they dealt with His words at the administration of the Holy Communion. They quoted them literally and combined them intimately with the visible act and gesture employed on the occasion when they were used. It was believed that in the Primitive Church and in the Universal Church these were the "sollennia verba" of ordination, and (all additions that they regarded as superstitious being removed) they concentrated the whole ceremony in the employment of these words with the laying on of hands. Thus Bishop Andrewes says that "Holy Orders" were given of old, and are given "to us even to this day, by these and no other words." At that time the fact was not known, which the investigations of Morinus subsequently revealed, that the primitive form of ordination—as is now the Oriental form—was *prayer* with the laying on of hands.* But as to the *intention* of the Reformers, and therefore as to the natural interpretation of our Ordination Service, I think there cannot be a doubt.

But one thing more, and this too of some consequence, remains to be added in reference to this our formula of ordination. It is not really the ordaining formula of the Roman Church at all. In that Church the act of ordination by the imposition of hands is followed by the commission to "offer sacrifice for the living and the dead." The utterance of the words, " Receive ye the Holy Ghost," with what follows, is subsequent to these parts of the Service. Thus the Reformers really made an extreme change in bringing those words of

* Bishop Andrewes continues : " Which words had not the Church of Rome retained in their ordinations, it might well have been doubted (for all their *accipe protestatem sacrificandi pro vivis et mortuis*) whether they had any Priests at all or no. But, as God would, they retained them, and so saved themselves. For these are the very *operative words* for the conferring of this power, for the performing of this act." I quote from p. 687 of the third edition of his Sermons, published in 1635. The second great work of Morinus, "Commentarius de Sacris Ecclesiæ Ordinationibus," was not published till 1695.

the Lord himself into combination with the imposition of hands, and with the commission "to preach the Word of God and to minister the Holy Sacraments." This circumstance is of no inconsiderable moment, when the whole subject is to be dealt with controversially.*

And that this is a perfectly fair way of looking at the subject may be shown by an examination of various documents connected with the Reformation. There was no disposition at that time to evade the force of those solemn words spoken by our Lord on the evening of the first Easter Day. The question which arose had reference, not to the weight and binding nature of those words, but to their interpretation. This might be confirmed by

* My attention was first called to this fact by Dr. Reichel's pamphlet, "Shall we alter the Ordinal?" (Dublin, 1872). His accuracy can be verified by an inspection of the Roman Pontifical. After the ordination is completed by the laying on of the hands of the Bishop and attendant Presbyters, and after power is given to consecrate the Eucharist, these words are addressed to them in a supplementary part of the service: nor is this supplement ancient. "Pontificale Romanum," (Par., 1664), pp. 42, 49, 53.

quotations from the various Protestant Confessions. But perhaps it is more to the purpose, and less commonplace, if reference is made to John Knox's Liturgy. "The Order of Excommunication and of Public Repentance," in that most curious and instructive composition, is very elaborate, and well worthy of being studied in its bearing upon our present subject.* It illustrates very usefully several points which have been under our consideration. Thus the cases with which it deals are *public*, as in the primitive times; and the discipline is exercised, not by an exclusive body of priests, but by *the Church*. "If a man be charged by Christ Jesus to go to a man whom he hath offended, and then by *confession* of his offence require reconciliation, much more is he bound to seek a whole multitude whom he hath offended, and before them with all

* "The Liturgy of the Church of Scotland, as prescribed by the General Assembly." Edited by the Rev. J. Cumming, 1840, pp. 140, 150. It is sometimes forgotten that the existing Scotch "Standards" do not, for the most part, belong to the period of the Reformation.

humility require the same." The form of absolution especially well deserves to be quoted and read—"If thou unfeignedly repent thy former iniquity, and believe in the Lord Jesus, then I, in His name, pronounce and affirm that thy sins are forgiven, not only on earth, but also in heaven, according to the promises annexed with the preaching of His Word, and to the power put in the Ministry of His Church." It is difficult to discern in this a weaker meaning than that which belongs to our Ordination and Visitation Services.

But the argument can be reinforced from a period considerably subsequent to the Reformation. It is a most remarkable circumstance that at the Savoy Conference no objections were alleged by the Puritans against our Ordination Service. There was certainly no hesitancy on their part in raising objections generally, some of them being of the most frivolous kind. In the exceptional absolution for the Visitation of the Sick they did suggest some alteration: but in regard to our Formula of Ordination they were absolutely silent. It would appear that, as regards this matter, those whom our modern Nonconformists regard as their spiritual forefathers were quite content. Nor can we be surprised at this, when we find in the Westminster Confession such a sentence as the following:—"The Lord Jesus, as King and Head of His Church, hath therein appointed a government in the hand of Church officers, distinct from the civil magistrate. To these officers the keys of the Kingdom of Heaven are committed, by virtue whereof they have *power respectively to retain and remit sins*, to shut that Kingdom against the impenitent, both by the Word and censures; and to open it unto penitent sinners, by the Ministry of the Gospel, and by absolution from censures, as occasion shall require."*

I will not attempt to decide whether the Presbyterian method of asserting this doctrine

* "The Confession of Faith, &c., with Acts of Assembly and Parliament relative to, and approbative of, the same." Edinb., 1836, p. 166.

in a body of abstract articles is better or worse than our method of interweaving our Lord's own words in our Ordination Service, and impressing their general meaning on the early part of our Morning and Evening Prayer. All I say is that the Presbyterian assertion is quite as strong as our own. For my own part, I venture to think that our General Confession and General Absolution are a most fair and a most wise exhibition of the teaching of the New Testament in regard to this subject. Our acknowledgment of sin here is public, and yet without scandal. Our assurance of pardon is personal, and yet without any secrets being made known, except to God, who really can distinguish the quality and magnitude of every sin. Each penitent can pour out through the words of this confession the whole tale of his sorrow and shame. The absolution comes in all its fulness and reality, because it is the absolution of God. We, the Clergy, are His ministers, not the judges of the Christian people. The blessing would be very great, if this controversy, which has been forced upon us, were to result in a more heartfelt value, and more self-abasing use, of these parts of our Daily Service.

CHAPTER IX.

PRACTICAL RESULTS.

SOME years ago, very soon after the declaration of the doctrine of the Immaculate Conception, I met at a friend's house in Paris one of the then recent clerical converts from the English Church to the Roman. Our conversation turned upon the new dogma; and I asked him some questions with the natural desire to know how one in his position viewed this fresh attitude of the Church of his choice. He seemed desirous to avoid the subject, and presently he proposed that we should take a walk together. This we did; and in the course of this walk, behind the Madeleine, he told me that he did not believe this new doctrine at all: that he knew it put the modern Church in contradiction to the ancient Church: —but, he added, his daughters being in the room when my questions were asked, he had changed the subject, lest their minds should be unsettled.

On this I ventured to ask him what course he himself took in the confessional, whether he acknowledged there this inability to believe what had been decreed and yet received absolution, or whether he withheld from his confessor information concerning what would be held to be a mortal sin. His reply was that, while residing in England (he gave me the name of the place) he made this incredulity known to his confessor, and asked whether in spite of it he could receive absolution; to which the confessor replied that this was not possible, seeing that such incredulity was resistance to the Church. In consequence of this, my informant told me further that he changed his residence to Paris, where he went to confession without making known this state of unbelief, in regard to which his conscience acquitted him of all guilt, and that he received absolution.

This anecdote appears to me to exemplify, somewhat forcibly, the deceptiveness of the system of Sacramental Confession, its liability to break down, and its tendency to do harm to our moral nature. Nor is it difficult to multiply proofs of this, drawn from many different quarters. Let the system be viewed on various sides, and the result is the same. As to anecdotes in illustration, some that are the most conclusive as arguments cannot with propriety be quoted—such as the coarse stories, for instance, which float about a place of pilgrimage like Einsiedeln in Switzerland, where the hearing of confessions is a systematic business. I will merely mention two circumstances which on two different journeys made a permanent impression upon me. Long ago, in Algeria, I was thrown in close contact with a French soldier, who was very friendly and communicative, and who was leading a life as bad as that with which we are too familiar among our English soldiers.

On my seriously begging him to consider the peril in which his soul was placed by such a course of life, he told me that once a year, before Easter, he did change his course of life, when he was preparing to confess and to receive the Holy Communion.* More recently, at Rome, an Italian layman told me that he obtained his first knowledge of some of the worst forms of evil, in early boyhood, through questions put to him in the confessional. He went in terror to his mother: and she spoke to his father, whose indignation was unbounded. A domestic shock of this kind sets the case of the secret confessional before us in an aspect which is very serious. But let these personal elucidations of the matter be now left on one side; and let us look more generally at results, as they appear to us probable from the very nature of the case.

In three points of view this system, as

* The decree of 1215, to which reference has been made above, requires that sins be privately confessed at least once a year.

contemplated from the outside, seems likely to lead to mischievous results. To the coarsely-criminal it must afford a most dangerous facility for lulling the conscience without true repentance: in others, whose spiritual sensibilities have been highly wrought, it must produce a scrupulous and morbid state of mind, unfavourable to the formation of mature Christian character; while in all cases it must foster the habit of leaning on human help to the weakening of the power of the personal conscience. As to the first point, let it be remembered how rapid and perfunctory is, for the most part, the hearing of confessions in Roman Catholic countries, and how easy a treatment, at wide intervals of time, seems to be accorded to "mortal" sins, which are certainly prevalent on a large scale. In the second place it must be carefully observed that, in such countries, though theoretically it is not necessary to confess "venial" sins, yet for the sake of spiritual benefit it is viewed as very desirable to confess them frequently. Hence there results, as we are told on very good authority, an unhealthy habit of self-inspection and self-torture, in order that the sins which are thus to be made known to the priest may be discovered, or perhaps invented. "There is a well-known saying among priests which exactly expresses the effects of this morbid self-searching. It is said that a man would rather be confessor to a regiment of dragoons than to a convent of nuns."* The harm of the confessional system, viewed on the first of these two sides, is that it pretends to heal by light treatment the wounds that are in danger of being fatal; the harm on the other side is that it "makes the righteous sad whom the Lord hath not made sad."† And in both cases a third result is sure to follow, which is singularly in contrast with the moral theology of the New Testament. Men and women,

---

* "To Rome and Back," by the Rev. J. M. Capes, M.A., (1873), p. 324. Perhaps it is in this form that, for the present, the harm of the confessional is most likely to spread among ourselves.

† Ezek., xiii. 22.

under this system, learn, more and more, to depend upon a conscience which is not their own. Advice that may furnish help to Christians to walk cheerfully in humble reliance upon God is one thing; recurrence to absolution, with satisfaction made through penance, is quite another thing. Where this is the rule of life, the dethronement of God's vicegerent within us, which is in fact disloyal to Him, is apt to be viewed as a high spiritual attainment. What can be more contrary to the teaching of St. Paul in regard to the conduct of the spiritual life? What can be stronger than his assertion, not simply of the supremacy of conscience, but of *each man's* conscience, as that which, under the enlightenment of the Holy Ghost, ought to be both trained and obeyed that it may furnish the law to *himself*? *

There are other aspects of the Confessional, of a darker character, which cannot with propriety be touched here except very lightly.

---

* See, for instance, Acts xxiii. 1; xxiv. 16; Rom. xiv. 5; 1 Cor. x. 29; 1 Tim. i. 5, 19.

In the last part of the sentence, which has been used as a kind of text for the remarks made in these chapters, Bishop Blomfield says that "auricular confession is the source of unspeakable abominations." These are very strong words; but they were used by a man of mark, holding a position of high responsibility, and in a document deliberately printed. Let us look at the words themselves.

An "abomination" is that which we dislike, that against which our nature recoils, and which we desire to remove far from us. The word so used is common in the English Bible —in the Old Testament we are told that "a false balance is an abomination to the Lord;" in the New Testament that "what is highly esteemed among men is abomination in the sight of God." But, further, we may look with advantage at the derivation of the word. An "abomination" is that which comes to us *with bad omen,* and is attended with portentous circumstances, like certain birds in the sky, which according to popular fancy are the precursors of mischief. I think we may justly use the word in its original sense, of that which is before our thoughts. The symptoms of coming evil in connection with it are so serious as to suggest alarm.

And the abominations of Auricular Confession are said in this sentence to be "unspeakable." This strong adjective may have been merely intended to be an expression of high indignation. But in the present instance it might with truth be literally applied. For, inevitably and officially connected with the system of Sacramental Confession, are some things of which the Apostle says that it is "a shame even to speak." If I were to translate here what can be read in Latin treatises on the subject, prepared for the use of the Roman Catholic Clergy, far more harm than good would be done, my readers would be terrified and disgusted, and I should be liable to be brought before the magistrate for the publication of this volume.

We reach here what appears to me one of the gravest parts of the whole subject. This system must be mischievous and wrong, because of the peculiar kind of training it requires for the Clergy. Assuming this training to be thoroughly serious (and I throw no doubt whatever on that point) the minds of the Clergy must be occupied to a vast extent with cases of conscience; and many of these cases of conscience involve details which are polluting. Observe that all mortal sin, which can be recollected, and which can be put into words, must be privately confessed. Observe, too, that there may be mortal sin in a thought, in a desire, in a look. Hence there must be a very elaborate and minute study to prepare for confessions of this kind. I frankly acknowledge that I do not see how, under such a system, this can be avoided; but this leads me to condemn the system itself. On behalf of the purity of the minds of the Clergy, the strongest protest possible ought to be raised against it. The Ministers of Religion, in the active discharge of their duty, come into contact with a vast amount of the practice of sin. Surely it cannot be an advantage to them to be saturated early with the philosophy of sin. The Clergyman's office and work should be a fountain and a stream of pure water, to cleanse and sweeten the bad lives of those around him. Can it be a benefit to him or to any one, that he should be the receptacle of all the foul pollution in the minds of his parishioners? This must be the result, if the system is carried thoroughly into effect; and if it is not carried thoroughly into effect, then there is trifling with mortal sin.

It will be urged that the private confession of sin and misery has been found in many cases to be of signal service towards the recovery from sin and misery.* That this is so, I have not the slightest doubt. There is nothing in this volume to contravene a fact which is gladly and thankfully conceded. To

---

* A few years ago some very serious letters—not at all more serious than the case requires—appeared in the "Times" concerning certain forms of vice which are supposed to be checked by private confession and private absolution. I confidently believe that if fathers would speak to their sons, at an early age, on such subjects, and then would kneel down and pray with them, more good would result than by the use of sacerdotal means.

those who are troubled with perplexities of conscience, even if those perplexities relate to trivial points,—to those who are under strong temptations, against which every possible help is needed,—to those who have fallen into shameful guilt, so as to feel as though recovery were impossible,—to such sufferers it must be very serviceable to open their griefs privately, and to seek Christian sympathy and spiritual advice, if only they go to the right person. But this I would add, that the true benefit in such cases is derived, not from absolution, but from sympathy and advice. The benefit may be found, and doubtless often is found, in the midst of a great system of sacramental confession; but it may also be found, and is found, without it.

It is the system as a whole, and the system in its mature form, against which the present argument is directed, for the purpose of suggesting caution in reference to the course on which many persons in this country are now entering. The fruit which has ripened, where Sacramental Confession has had the opportunity of growing in full luxuriance, is not concealed from us. Hitherto reference has chiefly been made to effects produced in the separate experience of individuals. Let us end now by calling to mind the testimony furnished by large communities.

Here again exaggeration must be carefully avoided. Contrasts are drawn, as regards civilisation, between Protestant and Roman Catholic countries, to the disadvantage of the latter: and, no doubt, the contrasts are, on the whole, in accordance with truth.* Still the law is not universal. Belgium may be adduced as an exception. Moreover success in this world's prosperity is not altogether to be taken as a test of moral superiority. When, however, we look below the surface, the contrast between countries which have long had the systematic confessional and countries destitute of that institution seems to become more marked.

At the "Old Catholic" Congress at Cologne,

* See, for instance, Lord Macaulay's "History of England," vol. i. pp. 47, 48.

in 1872, it was stated by Von Schulte, the President, that the purity of married life in Northern Germany was three times better than in Southern Germany :* and such a statement from so eminent a jurist, once high in favour with the Pope, after a judicial experience of many years, has a weight which cannot be gainsayed. The Papal States, which, if the confessional be the safeguard of morals, ought to have been the abode of universal charity, had, before the recent Italian changes, a hideous pre-eminence in murder. The comparison of London with Paris, of Berlin with Vienna, as regards vice tested by the usual statistics, leads to precisely the same conclusions.†

Or let the appeal be made, not simply to statistics, but to the general course of modern history. In Spain the Inquisition did its work thoroughly; no other form of Chris-

* "Verhandlungen des zweiten Altkatholiken-Congresses zu Köln," p. 87.

† In the work of the Rev. M. Hobart Seymour on "The Confessional" (1870), statistics are given which can be submitted to scrutiny, as being drawn from official returns. Ch. xii. and xiii.

tianity, except the Roman, was there, until lately, tolerated: the confessional there has been unfettered in its action: that country has produced some of the greatest writers on the subject: and what is the result? So in France. Those who opposed this system were slaughtered in the streets of Paris and among the valleys of the Cevennes. The Clergy had on their side all the influence of the Monarchy and all the enthusiasm of the sons of the Crusaders. Confession and absolution had the fullest opportunity for diffusing their benediction over the breadth of that fair land, and yet where does history record so terrible a revolt against all Religion as that which took place in France at the end of the last century? Or look across the Atlantic to Mexico and the South American Continent. A system so Divine, and acting so freely, and with so much power, and for so long a time, ought to have produced in those regions a paradise of holiness, corresponding with the paradise of nature which travellers describe. But this correspondence is not there to be found.

In proportion as this serious subject is closely scrutinised, the evidence accumulates that the restoration of Sacramental Confession through the action of the Established Church would be, not a blessing, but a curse. And yet the present assertion of sacerdotal claims, and that tendency to lean on outward supports of the religious life, which for the moment is fashionable, are sufficient causes for grave alarm. Already, too, we hear dark stories of clandestine confessions without the sanction of parental authority, and of questions which raise a blush being set before those minds which are the purest. Time can no longer be afforded for trifling with the subject. To all whose convictions are clear and strong against this new invasion of an old enemy, resistance, and resistance on the threshold, is an imperative duty.

Works by C. J. Vaughan, D.D.
MASTER OF THE TEMPLE.

Family Prayers.
Crown 8vo, 3s. 6d.

The Presence of God in His Temple.
Small 8vo, 3s. 6d.

Sundays in the Temple.
Small 8vo, 3s. 6d.

Half-Hours in the Temple Church.
Small 8vo, 3s. 6d.

Last Words in the Parish Church of Doncaster.
Crown 8vo, 3s. 6d.

Earnest Words for Earnest Men.
Small 8vo, 3s. 6d.

Plain Words on Christian Living.
Small 8vo, 2s. 6d.

Christ the Light of the World.
Small 8vo, 2s. 6d.

Characteristics of Christ's Teaching.
Small 8vo, 2s. 6d.

Voices of the Prophets on Faith, Prayer, and Human Life. Small 8vo, 2s. 6d.

W. ISBISTER & CO., 56, LUDGATE HILL, LONDON.

Works by the late Thomas Guthrie, D.D.

The Gospel in Ezekiel.
Crown 8vo, 3s. 6d.

The Way to Life.
Crown 8vo, 3s. 6d.

Christ and the Inheritance of the Saints.
Crown 8vo, 3s. 6d.

Man and the Gospel.
Crown 8vo, 3s. 6d.

Our Father's Business.
Crown 8vo, 3s. 6d.

Out of Harness.
Crown 8vo, 3s. 6d.

Speaking to the Heart.
Crown 8vo, 3s. 6d.

Studies of Character from the Old Testament.
First and Second Series. Crown 8vo, 3s. 6d. each.

The Parables Read in the Light of the Present Day. Crown 8vo, 3s. 6d.

Sundays Abroad.
Crown 8vo, 3s. 6d.

The Angel's Song.
18mo, 1s. 6d.

Early Piety.
18mo, 1s. 6d.

W. ISBISTER & CO., 56, LUDGATE HILL, LONDON.

www.ingramcontent.com/pod-product-compliance
Lightning Source LLC
Chambersburg PA
CBHW031337160426
43196CB00007B/707